The Holy Longing

The
Holy
Longing

Vera Graziadei

Matador
9 Priory Business Park,
Wistow Road, Kibworth Beauchamp,
Leicestershire. LE8 0RX
Tel: 0116 279 2299
Email: books@troubador.co.uk
Web: www.troubador.co.uk/matador
Twitter: @matadorbooks

ISBN 978 1789015 676

British Library Cataloguing in Publication Data.
A catalogue record for this book is available from the British Library.

Printed on FSC accredited paper
Printed and bound in Great Britain by 4edge Limited
Typeset in 11pt Minion Pro by Troubador Publishing Ltd, Leicester, UK

Matador is an imprint of Troubador Publishing Ltd

To the Source of the Holy Longing

Contents

Selige Sehnsucht

(The Holy Longing)

Sagt es niemand, nur den Weisen,
Weil die Menge gleich verhöhnet,
Das Lebendge will ich preisen
Das nach Flammentod sich sehnet.
In der Liebesnachte Kühlung,
Die dich zeugte, wo du zeugtest,
Überfällt dich fremde Fühlung
Wenn die stille Kerze leuchtet.
Nicht mehr bleibest du umfangen
In der Finsternis Beschattung,
Und dich reisset neu Verlangen
Auf zu höherer Begattung.
Keine Ferne macht dich schwierig,
Kommst geflogen und gebannt,
Und zuletzt, des Lichts begierig,
Bist du Schmetterling verbrannt.
Und solang du das nich hast,
Dieses: Stirb und werde!
Bist du nur ein trüber Gast
Auf der dunklen Erde.

Johann W. Von Goethe

Rendezvous

Melting ice
    crackles in a glass

        filled with crimson
           cranberry juice.

Completely alone
    in a beach café

        hidden from heat
           under a straw hat

I'm curious who
    has summoned me

        to this harbour
           framed by palm trees?

Engorged clouds
    hold their waters,

        a crawling crab
           catches my gaze

and disappears
        into a hole
                before I question.
The ocean
        swells and retreats.

I stay still
        and listen

                until its moans
                        envelop my silence.

I'm in labour
        birthing myself

                unto the shifting
                        sands of Time,

painfully mastering
        a traceless art,

                unravelling a code,
                        responding to an echo,

connecting

        to the lineage

that beckons

        becoming

                on a shore

                        of Life.

At the Golden Hour of Elongated Shadows

At the golden hour
of elongated shadows,
prompted by the
murmur of foam
on a grainy coast,
I summon up courage
and confess
my sinuous nature
to the sighing Ocean
with a rainbow halo:

Forgive me,
dear Father,
I've meandered
from place to place
person to person
thing to thing.
I wasn't fickle
just searching for meaning
It was slippery —
the more I tried
the quicker it would go.

I followed
the path fiercely
rising and falling
struggling with truth
and searching for love,
yet despite my intentions
I never succeeded in keeping
my serpentine path
straight.

The Ocean
in response
slaps me about
with muscular waves.
I submit to its force.
Then I notice a messenger —
a torn-away seaweed
that wraps around my ankles,
and clings to my toes.

I quieten down
and listen to its sermon.
Its undulating mercy
can sense my remorse.
Then it floats away.
Hysterical laughter.
A seagull.
It chuckles,
unimpressed by my tales.

This Ocean,
it squawks in mid-flight,
accepts daily
hundreds of wandering rivers,
narrow and wide.
Never have I seen
a curvy one rejected,
the more winding the better.
It adds to its charm.

Embarrassed,
I shake off the sand
and rise skyward.
How Ocean
delivers his wisdom
in subtle disguise!
Taught by a seaweed
and the far-seeing seagull,
I carry on following
my serpentine path.

Castaway

An empty space in a shard

                                 of a corroded mirror:

we won the battle

                             against the unrewarded part

and lost the whole.

                                   Where is the hero now?

Behind impressive numbers

                             and shining trophies?

There aren't any here,

                             so we haven't seen him

since the shipwreck

                                      at all.

Perhaps, like a coward,

                      he disappeared with the first

forceful gusts of Westerlies?

                    Or was disarmed and dissolved

by the embrace of the sea?

                      How could he abandon us

into this dreadful emptiness?

                    We fought for our ambition together

and now we are left alone.

The loss is severe.

Once the whole is gone,

the unconfined parts

are scattered around.

Impossible to find

without familiar signposts

on outdated maps.

It takes so much effort

just to ask these questions.

We are slowly deafened

by the symphony of our shame.

Scorched

by the memories

of the merciless tempest,

we nearly miss

the faraway calling

of a shell.

It instructs our deadened will

to walk towards it.

I obey.

                                               I am near.

It pulls me to its pearly ear

                       and listens hungrily

to my barren terrains.

                            It is not attuned

to any disharmonious noise.

                                   It pays heed

only to one thing —

                   the music of the eternal Now,

the voice of the Ocean

                                 that cups me

into a new clay

                              to be recalled

by the hearth of the Sun.

                          The shell echoes back

  what I have forgotten

    I grasp the humming sound

      like the saving ring

        in the sea of voices

          I once drowned in,

            now kept afloat

              with one string.

I kiss the rugged surface
of my marine sister
with a stirring of hope
that I can find the whole

attuning my steps
to the unstruck melody

reverberating
in my mind
as I wander
through a shoal.

Dragonfly

You've visited me
as an emerald dragonfly.
Your iridescence
gently floated near my eyelids
and they watered.
I saw your smile
in the fluttering wings,
before you hurried back
towards the glowing horizon.

Your visits are too brief.
I never have any time
to ask you about
your new beginning.
Are you happier now?
More satisfied?
Or are the new dreams
also leaving a frown
on your brow?

Please ignore my tears,
when I see you again.
Touch me lightly
and fly, fly away
into a different future.

One request:
one day
let me hear you laugh again.
It's your laughter
and laughing with you
that I miss so much,
especially during
these lazy days
when the lingering heat
lulls me back into
the labyrinth of memories,

where I chase you relentlessly,
as if trying to fool both of us
that you've only left for a bit
and about to return.

An Unexpected Gift

An unexpected climb:
the mountains exhaling the heat,
the lemongrass swaying gently
to the cadence of your verses.

An unexpected gift:
sea glimmers in the sun,
resembling your smile —
a passing moment of pure beauty.

An unexpected spring:
of words exchanging themselves
with a tender intention to stay
longer than their fragile sources.

An unexpected Life:
a mystery unfolding itself
to the music of the ephemeral wind,
infused with an impossibility.

Sea's Dream

there's no clear road from here
from the bottom of the sea

circles on the water above us
circles under our eyes

the morning after the ...
remember how melancholic

we were as we disentangled
from the seaweed and let

it float above us with sighing
bubbles released from our lips?

the mourning after we …
remember the music of our fingers

as they traced the matching wounds
that brought us to these depths

with their equal weight of understanding?

there's no clear road from here

not our choice: we were dreamt
by the sea that recognised in us

its unfathomable fullness.

Pulsating Heart

A pulsating heart
in the palm of a hand.
Recognise Love
by its state of
holy trepidation.

In the presence
of the Other
and the mystery
that unites the two,
offer gratitude
for the revelation.

More than a Muse

More than 'a shore for your waves'.
A cremation ground to burn
all your shadows down
to the bones of the
truth
that I hear
in the voice of your hands -
an exalted free flight of blackbirds
over the white snow of the mountain peaks:
the spring wind
through a window
gaping at the winter's
dead flesh.
In the furnace
of the combusting staves
ashes rise, reminiscing
of the disposed container.

The magician's touch
turns the clavicles' embers
to the oxidised clefs. Even closer
to the inward unfolding than gases
to the black rain
of my sobbing. Even stronger
than soul's gravitation to the miracle
of the imminent re-birth. Even now,
as I offer my words as a charcoal
to initiate your passage
through the trivial compounds
all the way into the capsule
of your innermost sound.

To Pasternak

How did it happen that you became
  my overwhelming ambition?
You, the honest witness of the tumultuous times,
enthralled by the beauty of dew-covered lilac?
The blaze of your intense gaze illuminates my trail
as I ramble through the labyrinths of your coded rhymes,
where you reveal the colourful secrets
of your black-and-white melodies.
You give so much, a lifetime is not enough to take it all,
but I'll take all I can, for this is how I'll carry the flame
until I have to pass it on through the veil of time.

Not a Lolita

You will not see me in the morning,
standing five feet seven in one sock.
I have no slacks, my school is over
and there's no "L" in my name to lull
your restless tongue — mine is a roar,
a raucous laughter of faith slipping
unnoticed through the fauces,
swirling your insides into a storm
to make each name a dotted line
with the silence on it. No more fears
where we rest in the arms of the fierce
noble-winged seraphs. Now we are
our own judges and juries. The murderer
is on the loose somewhere, yet here
the summer untangles thorns,
the heat answers solitary prayers.
I am your soul, your sin. Yet I am more
than just the fire of your loins. I am
the fire of your music and your verse.
I am the one you'll kiss at Eternity's gates,
once you fulfil your artist's vows.

The Way Back Home

I know how to find you
            in the city of star-gazing lovers;
through which cobbled lanes
                to chase you without a map.
Armed with an ice-cream
            and a marvellous melancholy,
I know how to smile at you
            to tame your exhausting beasts.
I know how to smooth the pain
        when the ancient squares applaud
the concerts of your silent screams
                suddenly replayed on a loop.
I know at what rate you pulse
        when making your way back home
from which you have been locked out
            by the sordid ancestral mistakes.
I know how to swing with you
        to the melody of forgotten dreams,
to be reborn in the summer's heat
            as everything but us is dissolved.

In a Small Town

In a small town, where solemn seagulls guard
a semblance of peaceful stability and familiar strangers fill
　　their days
with activities and celebrations, the point of which always
　　escapes you,
you choose to withhold your heart from life that holds no
　　meaning,
as you wait for the Right Time, not quite knowing what it
　　should be right for and whether
it will come, but hating the bell chimes and funeral
　　processions and even
the setting of the sun over the horizon, towards which you
　　still have an urge
to run before twilight, but you never do, out of fear: "the
　　gates should always
be locked before the dark and who will do it if not I?" I
　　foresee the day,
when upon hearing the evening cockerels, something in
　　you will crack
and, leaving your house door wide open, you will run out,
　　barefoot,
believing that if you chase after the Sun, you will remember
what you were forcefully forgetting all these years. You
　　will run, yet you will not

get far, as She will greet you at the first turning: your Muse,
your Ideal Love with burning sunset eyes, ruby lips, like
    cherries
of a long-awaited harvest, and long hair floating in the sea
    of the sky.
You will grasp at her, wanting to embrace her, but she will
    be transparent
like a ghost. "Not yet", she will whisper, and she will lead
    you
through the dark streets of your town, revealing to you
    every corner where beautiful lovers
gather into a night bouquet. "Love me", you will beg her
    desperately,
your blood flow electrified. "I always have and I always
    will", she will answer
as she dissolves into a mist. Like a madman you will sing
    about your loss
in every open late bar that will have you, crying out at the
    sight of kissing couples
in love, cursing destiny and dusty changing rooms,
    clinging to your broken heart, searching for her in the
    white mountains of other women,
who will follow you along your road until their skin turns
    crusty

from the salt of their tears. You will find some consolation
in the smiles

of hugging orphans and prayers of repenting criminals;
every outsider

will become a friend and every new grey hair of yours — a
love song,

until, all silver-headed and yearning for silence, you will
finally decide to return

to the fateful turning, where She will already be waiting
for you, all flesh and bones.

Lost for words, you'll have nothing to offer her but your
weeping.

She will soothe your aching skin with her embraces and
satisfy

your thirsty lips with the fountain of her kisses. "Why have
you forsaken me?",

you'll utter with your trembling voice. "I never have. You
dreamt me

with your mind", she will murmur, "but you had to make
me real

with the beauty of your heart's music." And only then the
time will be right for you to set out

towards where the sky and earth meet in a passionate
blazing surrender.

Fugitive Beauty

Fugitive beauté
Dont le regard m'a fait soudainement renaître,
Ne te verrai-je plus que dans l'éternité?
                              - Charles Baudelaire

It was just one moment of summer,
when walking down a cobbled street,
I felt I was someone else —
someone who hasn't lost home,
who still feels the sweetness of the soul un-split.
Someone who deals with time
without cutting it into manageable chunks,
without keeping memories in tins
dated incorrectly on purpose
so no one knows where I was and when
(even myself — that would be some luck!).
Someone who feels confident and complete
without anyone's applause,
who smiles at herself in the mirror,
who doesn't care about success and achievements,
who can be joyful during peace or wars.
Someone who always stands up
for the truth in her heart
without reservations and fears,
for whom Love has never become
a supporting act on the line-up,

who appreciates the value of friendship,
who serves and gives rather than uses and takes.
Someone whose lips are for kissing not for cursing,
whose body is for dancing and lovemaking, not
only for work and sex,
who continues to write love poetry beyond her
teenage years,
whose eyes never lost their light and heart is so
full of tenderness
it spills over at everyone who passes by without
any restraints.

It was just one moment of summer,
when I felt that I was someone else
and you were walking by,
and perceived everything that I can be,
and fell in love madly
and in that one single moment of passing
lived with me, deliriously happy, until your dying
breath.

Invisible Flâneuse

A wandering soul
with a heavy black kohl
around her eyes
slips into your mind,
gloating glossy reality,
as an invisible flâneuse.

She strolls down
the alleys of your
imperious desires
and dreams fuelled by absence
without an obscene response
to the insanity within.

She faces the ghosts
of fugacious women
with satin shoe straps
and tight leather belts,
wrapped around your mind,
and releases their grips.

You hoped it was
a square trap of desire,
but instead it's a
slowing down
of a lonely man afraid
of not going fast enough.

In a rapidly-metamorphosing
world, where there's only time
for love at last sight,
sustaining the moment
of finding is a
lingering farewell.

A queen of never turns you
into a master of always:
she's no fugitive beauty
whose bodies you stroke
with your eyes
in a scopophiliac bazaar.

She cannot be oppressed
by the male gaze,
searching for the culprit
of his existential
dissatisfaction,
she recognises its complexity.

She's a willing object,
finding her strength
in her presence
that dilutes too much 'I',
inscribing alterity on the skin
of ephemeral corporeality.

Desire is the desire
of the other for you.
She awakens you to yourself.
Her ever-deferred mirage body
brings coherence and unity
to your fractured mind.

She's not just out of reach —
she's lost from the beginning:
and utterly yours.
You are the sum of your losses
and she grows into you
by being your ultimate loss.

Light through the Blinds

I need to love you light
falling through the rolled down
blinds slicing your bare skin
into lines that I inhale
fulfilling my longing to unbind
you lead me to my limits
where I feel no longer able
to respond to the fears
of my mind your love
reaches further into me
tears stream as I expand
memories of depths I've lost
return to me in the corners
of your smile we're always
who cares if not now
in your vastness I have
grasped the softness of
my being belongs to you
unconditional invitation
to unfold the unconscious
layers into the now of

your black holes reflecting
my blue-green lakes
of tenderness this story
of holy co-emergence
evolves like a slow dance
to the rhythm of the sun
rising and setting behind
the mountains
of the eternal
together

With You

With you
        breaking waves
             at the speed
                    of unrestrained passion
With you
        serpentining
             through the saline waters
                    as untamed winds
                         tousle our hair
With you
        savouring the taste of sighs
             under the arched backs
                  of connecting bridges
                      no island left alone
With you
     putting on masks
         to reveal deep secrets,
             and once descended
                 to the depths of psyche
                    ripping them off again

With you
   delicately sculpting
      cries of seagulls
         above the rising tides
           as chiming bells
               punctuate the rhythm
                  of centuries' rocking

With you…

Wild Horse

The galloping of my heart towards You is as gentle
as that of a wild horse crossing a road in a misty forest
when the dawn is still whispering its spells and invocations
to the countless invisible creatures, dwellers of the night.

Its movement is elegant and precise —
there's nothing superfluous
in the daily self-unfolding of this intimate symphony,
which so easily intertwines with the humdrum of the city.
An eclectic composer always listens and
weaves into the whole
the rumble of the distant trains
and the sighing of the fallen leaves,
the children's laughter
and the chants of the anti-war protesters.

Anything can emerge as a note
of my longing heart's music:
a rickshaw horn, the repeating pleas of the *Big Issue* seller,
an announcement of a 193 steps climb at Covent Garden,
a Sunday morning chime of bells,
market traders' cries for fruits and veg,
football fans' cheers, dogs' barking,
people's voices, bird songs —
another note resounds as the rest of London's noises
fade into the background.

I hear you everywhere and I parse You at a gentle pace —
that of a wild horse crossing a road in a misty forest
when the dawn is still whispering its spells and invocations
to the countless invisible creatures, dwellers of the night.

The Full Moon

Immerse yourself in her milky fullness:
a voluptuous pearl, a jewel on your nights' crown,
she'll lead you to the land of your hidden shadows,
accelerating the expansion of your heart and mind.
Your roots will grow deeper into your life's foundations,
as your branches will extend under her vibrant light,
your racing heart will run towards her inner circle,
the cup from which you'll drink the inspiration for your art.
Your ground will shake under her incantations —
for a moment you'll feel like you've lost your sense of Self,
in your detachment she'll reward you with a sensitive ear
with which you'll hear the subtle messages
from the gods above.
She will dissolve your mind with her divine music,
your soul will resonate with the heaven's hum,
If only you'll immerse yourself whole in her milky fullness,
a voluptuous pearl, a jewel on your nights' crown.

A Secret Place

There is a secret place in you
where inner stars are born,
a nursery of nascent constellations.

There is a secret place in you
where a clover grows its forth leaf
and life flows easier through every dimension.

There is a secret place in you
which like an eye of a storm
is always calm even amidst a sheer devastation.

There is a secret place in you
where tears are sweet
from the joyful throbbing of the heart after its liberation.

There a secret place in you
where nothing can go wrong
and every step is guided by a continuous divination.

There is a secret place in you
beyond any language
where words resound in the air before their formation.

There is a secret place in you
which can be filled with Love
if only you'll believe in your own salvation.

There is a secret place in you
which feels like Home
allow me to dwell there sometimes for inspiration.

A Song of the Blue

Somewhere on an island in the middle of blue vastness
I'll build a humble home for you on a deserted beach.
No one will know aside from sneaky crabs and proud pelicans
about this shabby shelter from the wars
   and mayhem of the globe.
You'll reach this place on a floating raft,
leaving all your titles, toils, gold and guns behind.
The winds will soothe you with the whispers
   of coconut wonders,
as you surrender to the yearning waves of your ocean-mind.
At sunset we will walk along the shore collecting conch shells
into which we'll place our precious life stories
   and innermost dreams
until, caught in the crimson nets of the horizon,
we will retrace our past and future on the sandy skin.
And later, at night, when we become one
   with the celestial flow,
enveloped by our renewed hope and unruly hair,
we'll gaze at the sky's evolving love, the news of which
will then be spread by the singing frogs
   through the morning air.

Inspiration

I cast a spell over a scarlet flower,
 it trembles and the dew drips down its stem
into the earth that senses the magic
 and rouses storms over the seas and distant lands.
Nothing changes yet everything acquires a glow —
 after the tempest all creatures speak in a familiar tongue:
the morning birdsong stirs the immobile soul
 and luscious words flow from the unsealed mouth.
The crystalline air of the highest mountains
 descends into the corners of the subterranean caves,
the mind brims with infinite possibilities —
 its exponential expansion follows sublimating waves.
The inherent holiness of the unfurling creation
 commands the awe and gratitude to come forth
and bow to the one who's mere presence
 bestows the gift of the imminent inspiration's birth.

White Light

It reaches into you
                    deeply
like the branches of a lucid tree
                    a dream with roots
in your highest Self
        that doesn't exist
                    yet longs to be
            somewhere
        in the inner sea
    eroding the pain
            and suffering
uplifting the struggle
        to be free
            a memory of the world
                shaped
                    by the intimate reverie
        reaching to touch
            eternity
            that we have already surpassed
in the pupils of our eyes
        dilated by the force
                that underpins
                    the universe
    there's nothing more to us

                than a variation of a song
we'll seek its meaning
                                yet we are nearly gone
        out of Time
                                the sand is falling
            over our futile attempts
                        and despite the imminent loss
            I still yearn
                    for the ephemeral notes
                    of your being
                    play yourself to me
                        play
                    play day and night
                        as lightly
                    as we breath
                    as beautifully
                as I know you to be
                    as gracefully
                    as we are falling
                into the white light
                    of our ultimate
                        human
                        destiny

Bridge to You

How can I live in this world
when my being, incessantly,
seeks You everywhere I turn and,
upon not finding you, despairs?

How can I dwell in the land
of ego, lust and greed, when
I know of a place where You
inhabit all your Truth and Beauty?

How can I spend my days
accumulating honours and things,
which bring me but a drop of joy,
while your smile is a wide-open ocean?

How can I find strength to accept
that in this life I will never reach You,
and that I can only find traces of You
in Nature, Music and Art?

How can I calm this quivering
form that feels You at a distance
and knows that the only bridge
between us is this boundless longing?

The Space
Where You Are Not

I'll fill the space
where You are not
with words —
salacious,
sacred,
scintillating —
and fall into it like
a thirsty star
collapsing on itself.

        I'll sow longing
        of unabashed intensity,
        while saturating my pillow
        with paragraphs
        of imagined summers'
        storms.

        I'll swallow whole
        the invisible lakes
        at the bottom of which
        silky hands
        search desperately
        for oceanic salt.

Alone I'll wait —
on my knees,
crushing rosemary
with wet fingers —
for the season
to harvest
compulsive hopes
and fears.

And syllable by syllable,
I'll burn every
misplaced hope,
setting the
atoning horizon
with sacrificial fire.

Sacred Nonsense

For those who can make sense
of the sacred nonsense
scribbled on the scrolls of sleepless nights
I whisper the memory of a nascent sunrise
straight from the solitary corners of my heart:
after the long day of contracted monotony
be extremely transfixed by her milk and blood,
splashing unto the canvas of your reality,
pollinating Pollocks of your mind.
Laugh loudly if you're half serious —
make it the funeral music of your buried past —
tear out the currents of the holy passion
with your bare teeth hungry for the wanderlust.
Two expanding pupils — your paradise islands.
Swim to the treasure shores marked by the invisible cross.
No longer a stranger in your own body,
escape the familiar purlieus on the crest of the waves.
Dare to shake your untimely antiquity,
just for one moment — be who you really are,
this is your only life, embrace your sensuality
and twirl in the whimsical madness
under the aghast sky.

Magnanimous Mango

Some time in the heat of the summer solstice,
As you grow numb on your sampling quest,
It hails you from the hill that rises by the wayside —
The imperative presence overruling all ambitions and plans.

You are relieved when your imperious shadow disappears
In the penumbra of a densely foliaged tree,
Where miracles concealed are proffered to you only
And cravings — satisfied beyond any reverie.

The succulent flesh of each bestowed morsel
Blows up in your mouth, a pounding yellow lagoon,
As luscious orchestra enswathes your senses
In coconut, citrus, almond and vanilla keys.

The magnanimous mango purges you
    from sins and misdemeanours,
It wipes off the names of past loves and pains from your lips,
Releases the stuck notes of your deepest sobbing,
Initiates the re-birth of your wildest dreams.

An Appeal Against Pineapple

I am appalled
by its pretentious presence.
To look like an alien's head?
What does it think it is?

It appertains
to more approachable levels:
we all know that it grows
underground, like the roots of trees.

I appreciate
that apparently it has the power
to titillate our tasting apparatus,
but who cares?

I disapprove
of it as a dessert or an appetizer.
What's wrong with good old gala apples
and conference pears?

I apprehend,
(A chef's apprentice once told me)
that it has an inappropriate habit
of prickling hands and needling lips.

So I appeal
to everyone with sense and logic,
to keep away from this defiant mutant!
And to share widely these important tips.

Endless Dance

I'm charged —
on a balcony facing the splashing vastness —
to lean back on the singing of the frogs
and the aroma of the night jasmine
until my head spins,
the hands support me like strong roots
and the chart of my heart
bursts open to the past of the sky,
offering itself to the ancestral stars
to read me as their future.

In me they will see their death,
their meaningless floating as dust
for millions of years,
their slow ascent into the afterlife
as little atoms
which will then become me —
an assortment of memories,
pains
and longings —
gazing up to the source
for one brief breathing moment
until dissolving into the earth

as the stardust continues
its endless dance with Time.

I'm Listening

I'm listening
             to the glow
of the golden seed,
             the warmth
of the black earth
    which fills my mouth;

                    I'm listening
                              to the moisture
                    seeping through the pores,
                              the hunger of the roots,
                    discovering
                              the unknown depths,
                    the fearful whispers
                              of the buried bones
                    and remnants of scarecrows;

I'm listening
             to the softness
of the seeking steps,
             the lightness
of the remembering leaves,
             the ferrous taste
of the burning petals;

I'm listening
                to the landscape
that I've never lost
                the echoes
of the ancestral songs,
                the bitter salt
of the rebellious ocean;

I'm listening
        to the harshness
of protective stones,
        the tenderness
of the sulking clouds,
        the density
of the muscular rivers
        rushing towards
their goddess;

I'm listening
                to the baptismal light
of the midday dawn
    when the soundless darkness
of the day recedes
                to reveal that

I'm listening
            to the slowly
expanding
                sweetness
of the holy
            longing.

I Sit by the Sea
in a Black Peignoir

I sit by the sea in a black peignoir.
The stars watch my white face
mimic the melancholy of the full moon.
A pattern reminiscent of sweeter days
catches my eye on the surface of the water
and temporarily alleviates the pain of His coolness.
I'm waiting to perform the prescribed ablutions:
to negate, forget, delete all traces,
to harvest freedom with my wet limbs.
The raindrops smear my painted smile
and I'm overcome with grief again.
The fading flower of my heart will be reborn
in the womb of a swan!
Unrivalled in beauty, it will glide across the water,
glowing like the moon, and captivating the minds of
anyone, whose flotsam is in a tangled heap.
It will move through many silent windows of sleep until
His foot will appear, shimmering in the moonlight.
Reaching out towards it, the bird will flap its wings and
the blossoms will fall everywhere, gently kissing His toes.
That night He will inseminate me with his breath and,
satisfied, I will drape the sky with crimson tracery.

At the Pinnacle of Love

Paused at the pinnacle of love,
beholding its radiant, endless beauty —
beguiling like birth, intoxicating like death,
I breathed in centuries in one blissful moment
and saw that mountains are Earth's very slow waves.

One day I'll give birth to a delightful water creature:
a seahorse caught in my marine foamy nets,
floating above your snow-melted peaks,
by then submerged in my nauseous fertile depths.

The sky will be in decay and, apologising
   to the gloomy clouds,
Venus will swirl in its downward farewell waltz.
I'll keep my surface blank and swelling in a tide
will forgive the mischievous planet for every one
   of your crusty faults.

I'm still encased in days and nights, a seasons' collector
who marks falling leaves in autumn with salt granules
   on her cheeks,
I'll keep this summer-plucked flower
   between Dante's pages —
at the height of my herbarium's most burning prayers.

Touch of an Eye

I rub between the palms
the soiled leaves of autumnal letters,
the ones that cry with colour
from the dusk of their clinging
down to the dawn,

> where we lay
> festooned
> with freedom's feathers
> and fatherless fruits
> that you mistake for buds.

> what other flowering
> you need in autumn
> amidst the roots
> pulled from the ground
> and withered needles
> of dried blood?

> we sanctify everything
> beyond our reach,
> like these white hands
> made of pure snow —

you know that
they can melt hearts
at the touch of an eye?

Moonflower Woman

misgiving of fingers
in the pit of desire

unfurling deep fears
of the unconscious scent

a powerful phantasm:
the moonflower woman

untangling pocketfuls
of red-threaded strains

the song of cicadas —
a strike of existence

an essential passion
of powerless wind

a scarlet affliction
on hips of perfection

a kiss and a sigh
shredding shoreline with rain

a gleaming illusion
on the mirror of lessons

tidewaters resist
struck dumb by descent

of air infused with
a poignant significance

of a history of heartbreak
cached in a shell

prevailing confusion
at the bridge-way to beauty

a ludicrous strength in
the fragile event of

sunrise unveiling
forgiving embraces

in fields where the woman
can blossom again

Spring Blossom
outside my House

This is not an ordinary blossom.
Crowds rush by and I'm standing as if frozen,
            looking up at the epigraph to a different spring,
                into which I feel myself slip
            past the toil of hours that overlook my escape.
I'm elated by the tête-à-tête with my fate
                as Eternity's conspirator. Behind my back
I feel the presence of those who have given me breath,
        I'm exhaling for them and inhaling for those ahead,
who will pick up the blood's relay race
    on this Earth, which is now staring me straight in the face
through the hundreds of opening eyes.
                It's a game of recognition, I'm certain of it.
Never before have my own being's flowers been so revealed
                    in the nature of this city.

Two witnesses, face-to-face with the immortal in their intertwined veins.

Trees and people come and go, their vehement blooming always remains.

Where We Belong

I dread the passage
through the misty dust of dreams,
where the night murmurs infer surrender,
the sky's face is sprinkled with black powder dye,
and pillows are clouds,
exploding with anticipation of You
appearing in a kaleidoscope of echoes —
bloodshot-eyed, searching for peace
in my faveolate physique filled with fulmination.

And it fails you.
Again and again
in spiralling circles
of missed cues and
minute misapprehensions;
I can't scream because my mouth
is filled with compressed volcanic ash
and the moonlight is spilling over my sheets
and I'm drowned in the solemn frivolity
of its unearthly clarity.

Gasping for air.

What we hold in our palm during dark hours
is beyond our grasp.

The force of
the sun's smouldering incense:
only when poised in the light of day
hands grow into branches
and embrace the source.

Awake.

Awake is where we belong.

Awake.

A Return to Prose

We pasted ourselves seamlessly
   unto the savage grace of summer:
the memories of photos on the mantelpiece ceased
to delimit our senses yearning to break out
from the dark crevices of sentences
aching under the noon-sun.

We burnt until
the rain drops in our eyes
imbued the slang of sensuality
with a misleading feel of timelessness
that punctuated our togetherness with a sultry calm.

The carnivalesque attack of autumn caught us off-guard.

Shaken by the fall of pages, our poems
assumed a stance of awkward obscurity.
We've shed deciduous words, searching
for the new grammar of mythology
in puddles of silence.

Solitude laughed in gusts
and forced us back
to the fireplace
where

in the presence of photos on the mantelpiece we returned
to prose.

A Buried Bird

With a stifled cry
she has torn
the silk of the sky:
unfiltered light
fell on her porcelain face,
dissecting crystals
of dried up salt.

Intoxicated by
the amorphous despair
at the sight of the spade
tossed aside:
the bird was buried
still with a beating heart.
No sign, no cross.
Nothing to mark its years.

An extravagant weakness:
to tremble in anticipation
of hearing the strangely
familiar voice
reciting verses of spring,
while standing
at the gateway to Autumn.

Sharp blades
piercing the spines
of manuals on how to cut
fragile leaves,
the book on the deep roots
of wholeness
will be discovered
post-mortem.

The rattling sky persists,
dreaming of birds in flight,
to rescue her smile
from under the debris
of summer.

The black earth pulses now
with the swallowed life:
its petrichor breath
abridges the loss
by surmising
a cradling succour.

I lose her in the void of five o'clock

Dusk drips through the cries of crows
unto the ground which keeps me in its grip,
it merges darkness with my moving bones
and threatens to drown my companion in puddles.

I lose her when I move into the void of five o'clock
and as I stroll under the canopies of bare veins
I wonder what will happen
if I don't find her at the closing gates
leading to the lights and humming traffic.

She is the one with the turquoise eyes and long grey hair
that he beholds as she steps out from the cooled-down bath,
her long fingers travel on the ivory keys
and then his bare skin,
threading his wrinkles with the melody of surrender.

She summons cinnamon and fuses it
with the smell of the burning wood,
as she wraps his struggles and fears in her cashmere shawl,
the guardian of peace and the invoker of hope,
she heals him from himself with prolonged kisses.

Where is she now?
The talking shadows pass me unconcerned:
indifferent to the losses that are not their own.
"You are all just disappearing dreams", chants the wind,
as I hunch my shoulders to hide the rising sorrow.

Save Me

Save me from drowning in Lethe at noon,
the Lethargic hour of ghosts ascending stairs.
The day will come when, awake,
we'll swim and glimmer in each other's eyes
under the boughs of fir-trees.
For now we are the threatened species
with too much fire and earth,
praying for water,
while milling the dry air of days.
We're yet to suffer the martyrdom of the Moon
in the meadows someone will draw
on romantic paintings displayed in museums.
The lonely ships with lifted roofs
still sail the deluge of routine
and even grief betrays us amidst gross sense and custom.
Platitudes allow no peaks and
we retreat into solitude to converse with silence.
The counterfeit touches leave a shallow taste
on our skin, cursed by the summer rain.
Even if we were to dodge every drop,
we'd still have scars on our lubricious fingers.
We clutch and clutch but so much slips away.
We've sacrificed ourselves to endless
preparation and misguided striving
and even if we were to be re-born again,
it would take years to distill our essence
into a few seconds of crucial notes and words.

The Silence of I am

The silence of I am:
an unexplainable always
of the solitary sun
stamping the sign of ownership
on ever-shifting mountains
and solid sands
of the infinite landscapes.
An eternal tesseract
where a child, an adult
and an old woman
hold hands
oblivious to time
and change.
No past, no future,
no memories.
Only a tireless gaze
of the whirling depths
where dead stars
vibrate in unison
with their new-born
siblings
to create music
densified into flesh.

Special Gratitude To:

my children Giulia and Nikolai and my husband Robin
Dr. Rhys Tranter
Dr. Michael Korovkin
Sacha Wright Gottlieb
Alyona Schatzman
all the friends who supported me on my poetic journey

Notes:

The poem *Not a Lolita* borrows and re-composes language from the first paragraph of Vladimir Nabokov's novel *Lolita*

The poem *Save Me* is inspired by Ralph Waldo Emerson's essay *Experience*